Too Much Fun
to Be Legal

Poetry Collaboration

Nolcha Fox
Barbara Leonhard

Published by Garden of Neuro Publishing
A Division of the Garden of Neuro Institute
Poughkeepsie, New York
www.GardenofNeuroPublishing.com
Copyright © Nolcha Fox/Barbara Leonhard

ISBN NUMBER 978-1-962077-07-1
Cover Image by Sarah Erman
Cover Design Nanci Arvizu

Too Much Fun to Be Legal - sarcastic or spot on? Either way, it was insightful to take a metaphorical jaunt through the ups and downs of living, aging, and making choices in our world. You'll enjoy this delightful collaboration; they've produced and presented poetry in such a quick-witted way.

- Susi Bocks, author of *Every Day I Pause*

I am a fan of the individual works of Barbara and Nolcha, and together they made an excellent poet duo. *Too Much Fun to Be Legal* is a brilliant and engaging collaborative collection of poems that make you rethink the nature of your own vision and structure of the world. The witty and remarkable play on words is what sets this collection apart from other published poetry books.

- Michelle Ayon Navajas, Amazon Best Selling author of *I Will Love You Forever, Too*

Take this book in hand and find a quiet moment. As Nolcha Fox tells us in I'm no poetry groupie, "Images turn into / poems when / this old loner / basks in hush." With Barbara Leonhard's response, "My poems / are buried gems. / I dig in silence / searching / for each one," you will be glad they found them.

- Ken Gierke, author of *Glass Awash*

Acknowledgements

Nolcha and Barbara decided to collaborate after Nolcha's submission attachments to Barbara were mysteriously eaten by computer gremlins. Those gremlins were the topic of their first collaboration. It's been so much fun to work together, it shouldn't be legal.

In this book, Barbara's writing is in italics. Nolcha's writing is in what's left.

We thank our fathers for our weirdly dark sense of humor, appreciation of the absurd, and love of wordplay.

Thanks to the literary magazines for publishing these pieces in this book:

- Chewers *by Masticadores*: "Rocks"
- *Contemplate*: "Beyond the bend"
- *Doctor Funny*: "Cousin Trouble"
- *Extraordinary Sunshine Weaver*: "If I had an extra November day"
- *Gobblers & Masticadores*: "Creeps"
- *Hotel by Masticadores*: "Birth Name," "Cow Cud," "Fragile," "Hard-necked Porcelain," I'm no poetry groupie," "If I was only,"

"Living in Reverse," "Mischief," "My Wacky Friend, Grief," Party Hearty," "Sunset Flood," "Unconditional Love," "Wanna Play Marbles," Where's the UPS Guy," "Wouldn't it be great"

- *MasticadoresUSA*: "A portal opens in my closet," "Beyond the bend," "Dust bunnies dance," "I don't call it," "Laundry List," "Mischief," "No Words," "Spring Is Late," "The Secret Life of Socks," "Too Much Snow"
- *MiniMAG Issue 46*: "Mischief"
- *MuddyUm*: "Rate Your Pain from 1 to 10"
- *Roi Faineant Press*: "Road Trip"
- Thrush Press: "If I had an extra November day," "Life wanes"

Table of Contents

For those who have too much fun

A Portal Opens in My Closet

A shaft of shadow parts
like a curtain
to another dimension.
I decide to enter.
Will it be a nightmare
or an escape from conformity?

There's a hole
in the back of my closet
that spews out clothes
I wore in my dreams.
The closet rod is sagging
from the weight
of imagination.

My old clothes,
the small sizes,
meant for Goodwill,
balloon into buffoons
with snarky smiles.
My scarves take flight
like fairies. I follow.

My imagination
fits me better
than those Goodwill rejects,
and what was I thinking
when I bought them?
If the portal doesn't change them

into a bigger size,
they'll take a snarky flight
into the trash.

I chase the garment beasts.
Am I dreaming
or scheming
to find the gal
who used to wear size 6?
Or will the fairies
stretch my imagination
to fit my old hips?

The garment beasts
are giggling
as I bust buttons
pulling up these jeans.
The mirror cracks
up as I hear rips
of seams and dreams
of being a size 2.

I quickly gather up
my old wears
like they are firewood
and head home
through the portal
before it closes.
Mom said
I always carried
my weight well.

I will learn to weight
for that portal
to open again.

Beyond the bend

I cannot see,
I walk as someone blind.
The future is uncertain,
and I've left the past behind.

My past, a certain darkness.
What comes, in shadows too.
I pray for light to guide me,
my cane, my only tool.

Lamplight throws the shadows
to the corners of the room.
Light enough to see my Now
but not enough to leave.

The long dimly-lit hall,
a long haul to what's next
for this gray-haired girl
looking for a sunny meadow
and healing hot springs.

The future seems like a long haul,
but it is only steps away
to sunlit meadows,
hot springs,
and a nice hot cup of coffee.

Guatemalan course-ground
will remind me I'm still around.
Some chocolate and creamy ice cream.
A good book. Visits with friends.
Maybe the long haul
has a good end.

I am a coward.
The only good bend
is the bend in
my elbow.
At least that is one I can see.

Not me.
I'm so thinned skinned
that I have to wear sweaters.
But I know
my back is bent.
Maybe that's good
for hauling coffee
on the trip
to the light.

Birth Name

I was born a fiction,
a death, a hardship,
a drowning, cholera,
thunder, hail, rain.

No wonder I catastrophize.

I'm a dream, as well.
Each day, two suns wake me.
A warm hearth and hot coals.
I survive with an umbrella
and ibuprofen. At times,
life support.

Like hot coffee and chocolate.

I rebirth with dark coffee
and darker chocolate
I cradle in front
of a hot-coal
hearth every morning.
Each new self
should have a new name.
Wow, that's lots
of names to remember.

Does each new sun
have a name?
All the billions of suns.

All the billions of us.
Do mothers hear the sun
whisper our names?
Is the sun the keeper
of self?

Cousin Trouble

Cousin Rona,
the unwelcomed relative
who just shows up
with her bags.
She has a way
of getting under your skin.
You offer the couch,
but she takes your room.
Wants room service
and heating pads,
coffee, not tea.
Chocolate, which she immediately
spits out on your new comforter.
Chicken soup, homemade.
It's like you're boiling
the skin and bones
off your own body.

My cousin's name is Worry.
She brings a van full of her stuff
for just a weekend stay.
She says I have to toss my chairs,
my bed, and put hers in their place,
as mine is too uncomfortable
for her to oversee my fears
and take control of life.
She burns my calendar
that holds my chores and
plans for where to be.

She says she'll plan my life for me
as long as she's around.
She jumps onto my back
and drills a hole into my skull.
She pours herself into my brain
to make my life a living hell.

I hear that Rona and Worry
went into a bar.
Ordered Whiskeys on Cries.
Shit popcorn like spit wads
at customers.
Chased Margarita into the restroom.
Just wanted to be BFFs.
They were bounced out
like footballs.

Rona and Worry
found tickets to Cabo.
So skunk-drunk
they didn't see
those tickets were
no-return no-refund
one way.

Poor Rona and Worry.

Creeps

I don't have to watch
late-night fright shows
to get a bad case of the creeps.
Pretenders and swindlers
lurk on my computer,
preying on naivete.

The monsters in fright shows
dissolve at the ending.
I know I can sleep peacefully.
The creeps on the web
aim to get me to trust them
so I'll send them photos
or give them my money,
and shame me for being a fool.

Not to mention
the lonely men -
or so they pose as -
who steal accounts,
prey on my kindness
only to DM me daily,
calling me "dear,"
say they are God-fearing,
flag-waving patriots.
They ask for photos,
call on Messenger.
"How are you, Dear?
You haven't been in touch.

I'm so worried about you."
The ghouls haunt
my living minutes.
So, I ghost them.

Don't call me "dear,"
you don't know
if I'm a sweetheart
or a bitch. I know
it's prelude to
a smarmy move.
That's the first hint
I should ghost you,
feign that you are dead.
Don't reach out
when I go silent,
resurrect
what never was.
Don't assume
I'm simply busy.
Be a good ghoul,
go away.

Raised to be kind,
maybe too kind
to the forlorn.
But I'm no polite girl,
ready to concede or comply
to con artists, members
of lonely-hearts clubs,
predators posing in pretty smiles.

To thine own self,
not true, you!
Ctrl+Alt+Delete!

Diminishing

I grow shorter as I age.
High heels don't help
to reach that shelf.
I'll have to call
my husband.
He's a foot taller
than me.

Otherwise, I'm a monkey,
scaling shelves at the supermarket,
or using the grabber tool I was given
after my hip replacement
to snag containers.

Supermarket shelves fell down
last time I tried to reach the Spam.
Canned goods, bottles, scattered,
shattered down Aisle 3 and 4.
Now the market manager
won't let me shop without escort.
I just ride electric carts,
let someone else
do all the work.

Not just a monkey,
but a NASCAR wannabe.
I'm told I took off
at high speed
toward Aisle 6, toppling

a kiosk of cans of pumpkin
and evaporated milk,
quickly scattering
a queue of shoppers
and their carts laden with food
for Thanksgiving dinner.

Getting shorter doesn't mean
that I'm any less
dangerous.

Don't

I keep going
through bad choices
and wrong turns.
I don't give up.
I drive toward the light
in the tunnel,
even if it's a train.

Still, I hear myself warn,
Don't approach the train!
That tunnel might be flooded.
Just stay home and eat
some Ben & Jerry's.
Give yourself a pedi.

I scale every mountain,
manicured nails
finding every crack.
If I fall, I climb again.
When I conquer mountain tops,
I enjoy the perspective

and ice cream.

Careful. Ice cream melts
into the views. A sticky
waterfall you'll have to clean. Don't
climb anything. Mountain hikes

ruin manis and pedis.
Callous the feet.

I leave cleaning
up for others.
I keep going
out the door
for my next
far-fetched
challenge.

Relentless overachiever.
You thrive on stress.
Persistence doesn't
pay off. It lays off.
Walmart has a sale
on mini eclairs since
you don't do stairs.

Dust bunnies dance

in the corner, in shadows,
dreaming the animal
of rabbit, of dog,
of dandelion fluff
in the wind.

I give chase with a broom.
They hop under my bed,
huddle behind the headboard,
dust my dreams,
munching on my nightmares
like they're old carrots.

I think they are rabbits.
Besides munching nightmares
like carrots, they breed,
having litters that litter
the floor with more dust.
I vacuum, I sweep,
but they scatter to shadows,
come home when I'm
trying to sleep.

They conspire with spiders,
creating dusty webs
that tangle my life,
trapping me
as I hunt their spawn
behind curtains and books.

Perhaps they remind us
that we will soon join them
as dust that returns
to the earth.

Fork

Two roads before me,
both carpeted with dead leaves,
gloomy under gnarled trees.
I don't know where they go,
I bet the destination
is the same. Or not.
Does it even matter?
I stab my apathy sandwich
with this fork in the road.

How odd
- a-PATH-y
g-LOOM-y
sand - WHICH?

WHICH sandy beach to walk?
Do I look telePATHic?
Do I look like I make decisions?
A storm LOOMs, better pack before it hits.
I'll decide where to go at the airport.

My documents, mismatched and expired.
My ticket says, "to the moon and back".
My suitcase, full of Swiss cheese.
The plane, a prancing cow. I hold on
for lift-off. 10, 9, 8, 7, 6, 5, 4, 3, 2, 1.

Zoom!

Fragile

Be careful what you say.
Sharp words will prick and pop
my heart today, scatter roses
on the floor.

Petals here. Petals there.
Tiny petals everywhere.
Broken heart. Broken care.
Petals wilt in my despair.

I put the pedal
to the metal,
can I drive away
from pain?

Harsh words drive me away.
I need a new place to stay.
Escape I must in all this dust.
My heart ablaze, my metal rust.

Leaving doesn't
leave the pain.
I pack it in my suitcase.
I may seek refuge
somewhere else,
but I'm still torn and broken.

Escape is just a band aid.
True healing is delayed
of the torn and broken heart.
I don't know where to start.

Freedom of the Body

Unshackle me from
pantyhose and heels,
from suits and ties,
from heavy bags
and briefcases
filled with everything
important, so we think.
These costumes
only serve as weights
to keep a work desk
in its place.

May my body
bend in breeze.
A stem in the sun,
swaying to the surge
of wanderlust in bloom
to the tunes of the clouds.
rooted in the fire of joy,
not anchored to the pyre of blue light.

Let me sway naked
in front of the mirror,
laughing at aches and age,
smiling at the splendor
of my imperfections,
happy for sun on my skin.

My true self is a cumulus
span of sky, steam rising
from a steady stream of latte.
Clouds won't make me prettier,
just more radiant as I dash
from my desk to Dunkin' Donuts.

I'm a Dunkin' Donut,
my skin the sheen of latte.
C'mon guys,
I'm a delight to bite.
Eat me.

Get Moving!

My iPhone Fitness App
complained that I didn't close
my Move Ring today.
"Just one more chance.
Get out of the moo moo.
Into your tennies.
A jog around the park.
A hike at the river.
Now!" It says.
"Get moving!"
What's stopping me?
Let me tell you!

My tree ate the Internet this morning.
All I could do was stare at the screen.
My fingers froze above the keyboard,
typing did no good.
I forgot to eat and drink, to dress, to bathe,
waiting for the screen to glow.
How can I move on with life
when I am not connected?

Arthritis is eating my joints.
Even if I'm connected,
my fingers can only crawl
across the keyboard.
How can my failing knees
and collapsing back
handle a marathon?

Ten thousand steps a day.
Not happening!

My body only lets me move so much.
My brain, another thing.
My thoughts leap to conclusions,
fly fast out the window.
Can you measure thoughts instead?

At least I can remember
to carry my thoughts!
Though my memory
has slowed down
to what rings true.
But I don't carry my phone
around the house
to what rings "Move."

Glutton

I'm obese with information overload
from people I don't recall.
My laptop beeps to burp up
messages beyond its memory.
My brain too fat for liposuction,
too much coming in too fast.
Unsubscribes ignored.
I don't know how to
unplug myself from
this electronic addiction.

My dimpled Word belly
gets in my way
when I sit down to tweet
and reheat my tweets as treats.
I fill my spreading thighs
with poetry groups on Facebook.
Instagram is a bit sticky for me.
I've become a mastodon
with all the time needed
just trying to figure out Mastodon!

There is no diet
to thin my whim for gossip.
I must eat and eat and eat
the latest news on all the folks
I plan to never meet.

Yet share, share, share
with some I never care for
unless we make connections
by gobbling up emojis
sprinkled with fake Splenda.
Our bitmojis fatten up.
Blame it all on glutton. But
they're just bots from Putin.

Bots shove info
down my throat,
make up fake news
about me.
Then they share it
with the world.
I find myself on TV.

And then in the tabloids
with the Royals
speaking of crowns
and all their toils.
Then I met Mary,
who was quite contrary
until Jack awoke from his nap
and carried a rabbit pulled
from his hat up the slack
into the sky. Then everyone clapped
to the truth of all that!

Where is the fat farm
to empty my head
and teach me to
play endless Bingo instead?

Hard-Necked Porcelain

I'm hard-necked,
stiff-necked,
denser than ceramic.
I easily crack
under pressure.
On a good day,
I'm pungent.
I season conversations

with my hardneck porcelain garlic.

My ivory face cringes smile.
My eyes neither blink
nor cry black.
Even my limbs fail
to compromise.
I sit and watch.
Watch.
From the chair
across from
your bed.

Yes, I watch you. Watch.
Every move you make
is etched into my skull.
You will crack
long before
I do.

Her eyes sparkle

blue, exit wounds
of sunlight
on this cloudy day.
"Can you open this?"
I take the jar from
fingers bent cement,
unruly, swollen,
straying from
its thumb.
Her smile
at the open jar
at odds with
constant pain.

Though her joints
swell with menthol,
her eyes,
icy hot
blue-emu
all to themselves,
salve my grief.

The ointments and the medications
multiply with every year.
As joints break down
and organs rot,
I understand why
God invented death.

I can relate, Sis.
My body, an old chassis,
needs work.
A leaky battery,
rusty rivets,
screeching steel.
My tires're gonna
do the splits
and drop my engine.

If only I could buy
a newer model to replace
this worn-out junker,
life would be just grand.

If only the heart
could renew its lease
every two years,
the eyes never dim,
the warranty never expire.
If only.

I don't call it

insomnia, I call it
inspiration, I call it
catch that star, I call it
lightning

to the brain.

and I don't call it
anxiety, I call it
butterflies, I call it
passion

in the heart.

I don't call it
on the phone,
I don't send
an invite.
Insomnia
a constant guest.
If only she could cook.

If only I could eat
something good
for my tummy.
The butterfly stew
on my daily menu
is inedible.
Those thin wings

get stuck in the teeth.
Is it passion
or heartburn?

Maybe I'm allergic
to butterfly wings.
Or maybe it's insomnia
that makes my tummy
toss and turn.
I wonder if I'll ever
fall asleep,
or find a better cook.

A half-baked meal.
A half-baked night.
What do you call a chef
with buttered wings
on the fly? Don't
call her Sous. She's
de partie.

I'm looking

for that unexpected clue
that will point me to the
secret door with a lock
that matches one
of these keys
in the drawer
where lost things
magically appear.

Like the shards of my soul
lost in traumas.
Some left to haunt
old homes, playgrounds,
hospitals. How to rescue
those missing pieces
of my memory?

Do I rescue what I've lost,
or do I let my soul shards leave
and travel with a lighter load
to the secret door?

Will they find their way
without me? Tapping the cane,
too blind to see the next step
or find the light switch?
This life shattered my mosaic.
Can I enter this mystery, broken?

I'm a 1,000-piece puzzle
with parts of me missing,
a mosaic with shattered tiles.
Either I mourn what I can't replace,
or make myself a different design.

I'm no poetry groupie

even though I love
to meet online with
fellow poets, love
collaborations.
Words flow best
when I'm alone.
Images turn into
poems when
this old loner
basks in hush.

My poems
are buried gems.
I dig in silence
searching
for each one.
I polish
their rough contours.
Hold them up
to the light.

Except for the really
bad poems.
I hit them on the head
with a shovel
and bury them
in the backyard.

Which is a mistake.
Once I didn't consider
the gas line. But at least
only my bad lines
went up in smoke
that time.

If I had an extra November day

I'd play in the leaves
I piled up the day before,
eat another slice
of pecan pie.
I'd light the candle
in the pumpkin
one more night.
How nice to have
an extra day of fall
before the winter
lays its icy hand upon
the barren branches.

A day to lay aside
those things I've buried inside
my closets, drawers and cedar chest.
Forgotten bits of my life,
bundles of burdens,
to stow into recycling bags
as I've outgrown my past.

All those things I've stuffed
inside my chest, the past
that weighs me down,
I open my mouth, let fly
what I've outgrown
on this November 31.

Let fly like bluebirds
singing hope and joy
on this mysterious day
suddenly visible.
Just for me?
A gift of extra time.

If I was only

brave enough
to make mistakes,
I would live
in Oregon now,
alone except for
a Siamese cat,

and I wouldn't be
a writer.

But can we count our
chocolate-covered
could-haves
and wishes-smothered
would-haves?
And pick our if-onlies
like they are peonies?

My coulda-woulda-shouldas
are tulip bulbs I plant.
Mistakes are lilac bushes
that color skies with pink.
Dogs and husband
dream of chasing
chocolate-covered
Siamese cats through
peonies in spring.

My dreams come true
in my tabby cat's eyes,
crystal balls
that hold my breath
as I see what can be.

My crystal ball
is smudged and cracked.
I cannot see the future.
I can only guess my best
with each step in the present.

Then why do we banter
about what could have been?
We breathe in the Now.
Living in the past
is a sign of grief.
And the future,
worry.

Laundry List: A Zuihitsu

Wash out my mouth with soap
(I can't believe I said that, yes, I can).
Floss my brain of moldy
thoughts and stale crusts.
Open the windows of my eyes,
let spring breeze stir up the dust.
Wash those winter clothes
and pack them in the back
of my thoughts.

Recycle those bags
under my eyes.
Stick my back in the corner
like a cane.
Pluck my hair
for blue jay nests.
Let's eat crow for dinner,
and when we're thinner,
we can jog our memory.

Figure out how to reverse time,
to become a child who dances
in the sprinklers, jumps
in puddles when it rains.
Or, just settle for
juvenile delinquency.
Do old people go to jail
for throwing spit wads
at the ceiling?

Or spit wads at dust bunnies
wearing my half-eyes readers
just to be mean?
Who put my memories
in the gutter?
Last I looked,
a spider wove them
into a web of time.

A spider web that
holds our lives
together, fragile.
how easily a careless
tear can plunge us
into chaos, never mind
the hearing aids
and glasses that we
wear as armor,
fighting to the end.

To the end of time?
The end of the line
off the edge
of the last multiverse?
Watch us spiral
into a spill of verses
with no rhythms or rhymes.
Just the memory's flatlines.

Flatlines,
bad rhymes,
verse averse.
This is a list
for a stinky poem.

Life wanes

as sun's weak touch
caresses my cold skin.
I barely hear the talk of who
did what to whom
I know I'll leave behind.
The thoughts they cannot utter now
will flower when I'm gone,
while some will keep in lock and key
the harm they think I've done.
My breath slips slowly from my chest,
as slip my thoughts of how I've lived.
I recall as Death stands by

I drank 5,000 cups of coffee.

But even caffeine
won't kickstart my heart.
Death sits across the table
holding my legacy
and peels open the book of my life
like it was a dry Minneola Tangelo
to check and double-check
my purses and curses.
I hold my face of frowns
in my weeping palms.
Really, Death?
No good news?

I offer Death
some coffee and cake.
We compare best buys
on books and on purses.
My chin on my palm,
I admit I'd spend more,
but bills won't be paid if I do.
"Enjoy life, don't worry,"
Death says with a smile,
"Debt won't be your problem
much longer."

When? I wonder.
Death dives into
"The Days of Our Lives".
Stops at page X to a higher power.
Sooner or later.
I'll need a new coat?
A gown? Glass slippers?
It's come as you are
through the tunnel of light,
across the River of Forgetting,
and into the blazing blue eyes of God.

Living in Reverse

I now admit I can't live like
I did when I was younger.
One-level living suits my knees
much better than three stories.
As I pack, I find too much
to move to smaller quarters.
How did I stuff
forgotten stuff
in every nook and cranny?

My pea-green canvas
Girl Scout bag,
holding my mischief.
My lineup of Simpson family dolls,
gifts from Burger King.
Music CDs and exercise DVDs
I can no longer play.
A half-set of expensive china
from my husband's prior marriage.

We only kept the china
'cause it made his ex-wife mad.
I can really get her ticked
by giving her the half-set back,
as well as all my hubby's stack
of 300 souvenir T-shirts.

Those dishes just gather
dust in the hutch.
The blue and white stoneware
from my prior marriage,
now cracked and broken.
Speaking of stones,
what do I do with my husband's
bags of agates, petrified wood,
and rocks from his river walks?
Lay a new patio?

The trash man knows to pick up
all the treasures we don't need
when we're out buying boxes.
We'll throw whatever we have left
into a backyard bonfire.

The clothes, the old editions
of unpopular books,
the family letters,
moldy from that water leak,
the tablecloths stained
from holiday dinners -
all can burn.
But memories
cannot.

Mischief

The gremlins ate my links for lunch,
I cannot get to Amazon.
Now they're eyeing photographs
I stored on my computer.
Social media may be next.
Will I be erased?

They spoon stupor
into my coffee.
Stir in rancid algorithms.
Claim my poems
are composed by Google laMDA.
My hard drive in lockdown!

Gremlins giggle
as my emails
evaporate from sight.
How will they know
I'm meeting their demands:
lifetime chocolate
in exchange
for leaving me alone?

My new email threads,
their tangled jewelry.
My book links,
their phishing lines.
I feed them Snickers,
they serve up Spam.

I troubleshoot,
they duck.

Gremlins angle with tangled
jewelry and phishing lines,
anything to catch attachments
and my attention.

Hungry gremlins eat attachments
like they're computer chips.
They gobble rich text,
especially my poetry
gone like a snack.

My poems are not
all you can eat.
Gmail is not
a free buffet.
Instead of munching
bits and bytes,
eat real food instead.

Like the cookie crumbs
between the keys.
Flood them out with my coffee?
Not going to fall for that one again -
or hitting factory reset on my iPad
without cloud backups
when you gorged on my WiFi.

I take my hard drive
to repair the damage
you have done.
The shop will suck you out
and take you to the shelter
for adoption.
Your new pet parent
won't be me.

My Body Betrays Me

My body refuses
to read the fine print
that I'll never be
older than 10.
I'll always
play hopscotch
and slide on
wet sidewalks,
and run through
the puddles
when clouds pour
down rain.

I still love sitting
in meadows of wildflowers.
Taking drives to the wetlands
to count the deer,
herons, and pelicans.
Dancing with the murmuration
of blackbirds on plowed fields.

I want to be outside
to sit in the meadows,
to drive to the wetlands,
to dance in the fields.
But I get too cold,
even with layers,
and I can't be late
for taking my pills.

I sit in my warm house
and drink some more coffee,
glad that my dreams
will never get old.

I'm well-dressed
for my dreams.
In bed, I wear layers -
a long gown, a t-shirt,
leggings and slipper socks.
I await the Sandman.

The Sandman brings
sweet sleep and dreams
every evening,
restores my old body
and brings me new hope.
I wake in the morning
to see a new sunrise,
eat a bran muffin,
and welcome the day.

My Wacky Friend, Grief

I find her in my attic,
rummaging through an old cedar chest
filled with broken hearts.
She's donned Mom's
silky wedding dress.
But on her head,
Grandpa's fedora. Her shoes,
Grandma's slippers.
In her hand, some letters
tied with a red ribbon.

I find her in the breakfast nook
crying over spilled coffee,
or drinking all the liquor
while paging through
old photo albums.
She wails because the loss is new,
years later wails because
she cannot remember.

She pours him
a cup of coffee daily.
Places it on an altar for him
next to a photo
of a dashing youth.
Lights a small candle.
Another day sips away.

The coffee gets cold.
The picture fades.
The candle burns out.
She looks at the altar,
can't remember why it's there,
but knows someone is missing.
Time for another cry.

Why is it that
some days are sunny?
Some days are bleak?
Some days grief
sleeps or just sighs?
Why is it that
my wacky grief
never dies?

No Words

I'm just an old lady
seventy and counting
if I want to complain
all I have is words for poems
and today again -
after yet another mass shooting -
angry words that weep blood
onto your closed eyes
as you are shooting blind
at families in a mall
party-goers at a bar
people in their church
children playing possum
under their desks
because you have
no sense no humanity
no words
to describe your malaise
only bullets
- and I too am left speechless
searching for words to describe
my state of utter despair
when calls for prayers
fall on deaf ears
and children's lives count less
than a round - there are
no words
to grieve this void

Not too tall or short,
not too thin or fat,
he only spoke when
spoken to, his voice
not loud or soft,
his face the kind
you look right through
when walking in a crowd.
At gatherings, he blended
into wallpaper, chairs,
and rugs. His friends
forgot his name, forgot
to call, they barely
knew him anyway.
Nobody was prepared
when he went into a mall,
and opened fire on the crowd,
then killed himself for
one last chance to
be noticed by the world.

The invisible one
whose pain dynamited
our loved ones
with terminal velocity,
the visceral effects, ready
for the macabre
on YouTube or Tik Tok,
scarring our lives.
No winners. No stars in this show.
Only victims.

Out of Office re:

your inquiry about your migraines,
the broken appointments at rehab,
the strange lumps on each elbow bone
how they flared up, at the same time -
each with a little white eye in the center -
and dried up into a scab. Is it cancer?
You called again re: the way
he brushes you off, like you're a fly.
The way the trees are bending
in the heat, thirsty for answers.

You called re: why you couldn't
make it to the office today.
The parking spaces too small
for your car that expanded
to fit your yoga mat and coffee cup
is not a valid excuse.
Please take the bus.

Your inquiry re: the refills
on your narcs. Wasn't the hysterectomy
in 2006? Oh, you mean the hip replacement
in 2011? Re: your appointment about
the knee replacement.
What do you mean
we aren't on the bus route?
You work here.

I don't work here anymore.
Did you not get my
out of office re: I quit message?
P.S. re: the bus:
Due to road construction,
the bus stop
is now two miles away.

Party Hearty

Rona woke up on
the right side of the saddle.
Felt hoarse. Coughed up phlegm
the color of runny yolks.
"Good day for a party. They love
my infectious humor."

Worry woke up on
the wrong side of the bed.
Snorfed up dust bunnies
and family ghosts
hiding under the bed.
Crawled out, white
as a sheet.
Told Rona she could party
for Halloween.

Rona's impatient.
The trail to October
is long and lonesome.
But the veil is thin on
All Hallow's Eve. The Rakes,
witches, night crawlers, skinwalkers
can hitch up their brooms.
Set huge bonfires in the Holler.
Dance with feral forest folks.
Make s'mores.

Worry tells Rona to hop on her broom,
pick up some coke and some rum.
Worry can cough up
some ice from her veins,
and vomit up
yesterday's popcorn.

Rona put Worry back to bed.
A fever of 105. Hallucinations of
partying hearty with the damned.
Horse races with google gremlins
wearing email attachments.
"Rest well. Worry. Bigfoot's pedi
can wait."

Payne Comes for Tea

Uninvited again.
Slaps my ailing knee.
"How's it goin'?
Not up and about yet?
How 'bout a jog
around the block? What!
Can't do gravel for weeks?
How can I help? Dishes?
Oh, my arthritis is killing me!
Maybe next time. Can you spare
some Tramadol?

I serve Payne
headache laced with Toradol
on a plate.
I drop the napkins
to make her
gravel on her knees.
Before she leaves,
I give her a doggy bag
of arthritis and sick stomach.
I hope she enjoyed her tea.

Payne arrives
with her sewing kit.
Saw a video on YouTube.
Now an expert. Sticks needles
into my surgery knee.
"Acupuncture?" I ask.

"What's that? I just need
a pin cushion for this thing." —
The thing she sticks in my mouth
to keep me quiet.

I am not quiet when Payne arrives.
I growl, I snarl,
I'm a woodsy thing, shaggy,
unmanageable.
I bite, I tear.
Payne is a
pincushion.

Payne says she comes for tea.
But she simply comes for me.
Again and again.
No matter how many goodie bags
of Pepto Bismol, baby aspirin, floss
I send her out the door with. But
an apple a day won't keep Payne away.

Rate Your Pain from 1 to 10

It's 15! Throbbing, stabbing,
radiating. It's a 300-pound man
on my back. My legs shake
from the weight. My knees buckle
as I slog along. Breathing
is a chore. Rolling over in bed
dislocates my dreams
to recover.

My pain is off the scale.
My pain stopped
rating itself
and just showed up instead,
with a moving van
and a nasty attitude.
I think it's here for good.

I bribe my pain. Go away,
and you'll get chocolates
with love songs
on the wrappers.
I promise that I will
give up Diet Colas
and cheese on broccoli.
Hell. I'll give up broccoli!

Pain can't be bribed
with chocolates.
It doesn't believe

I'll eat better next time.
Never mind, pain.
I'll eat the chocolates myself.
You're too big anyway,
and you need to go
on a diet.

Road Trip

The moon is a vacancy sign, and I want to pull in for a rest. But the parking lot is full of stars, their headlights blinking through the dust my tires kick up. No room, no room. I must drive to escape the darkness, a mouth ready to swallow me whole from this lonely road. I fade into the crumpled map in my hand. No Google Maps police directing traffic on my phone, this is a moment of silence.

Forced to proceed, guided by the eyelids of shadows. Slits of moon gaze. Night eats the gas, and I hope to make it before dawn. Some food left. Why don't I plan? Nut bars, a half thermos of coffee, sliced apples. A short trip, they said. But the road stretches like a rubber band, ready to snap. The farther I drive, the farther away I feel. In the woods along the road, eyeshine follows me into a mist. And then a thick fog.

A hazy amber halo shines through the fog. A gas station. I pull in for gas, coffee, and something to quell the queasiness in my gut. Maybe hunger, maybe anxiety. I'll know which in a few minutes. The counter guy asks how much gas. His skin is sallow, his face gaunt under the fluorescent lights, his eyes shining emerald green. I think zombies, and my stomach does a backflip. Definitely anxiety. Driving at night is another one of my terrible ideas. Just as I'm hopeless at planning, I'm hopeless at not listening to the warning bells vibrating this saggy old body. I pay for a jumbo-size coffee, some candy bars, and gas. This road will either boomerang me back home or snap me to my destination.

The fog finally lifts like a balloon rising. The road darkens into the shadows of trees lurching toward me like zombies, but do zombies' eyes reflect headlights? I shake off the image of the man at the gas station. I wouldn't be here were it not for my grandmother passing, and her memorial service is on Sunday. I'm not used to traveling alone, especially at night. Cataracts. Up ahead I see someone walking alongside the road. A young girl? Out here alone at night?

"Are you OK? Do you need a ride?" I notice that she's shivering in a red windbreaker.

Her car has broken down. I don't recall seeing one. Maybe the fog swallowed it. "I could use a ride to my grandmother's."

"You too? Hop in." I brush the candy wrappers off the passenger seat.

In the washed-out glow of the overhead light, her thin, pale face looks barely held together, a vanilla cake with the top layer sliding off. Something about her is familiar. I don't know what. My stomach somersaults.

"Wait a sec," she looks down, fishes in her pocket.

I raise my hands in surrender. "Take whatever you want, just don't hurt me."

She looks up, her feral eyes glowing green. And morphs into the gas station counter guy. "You forgot your change." He puts a quarter and two dimes on the dashboard.

The counter guy opens the car door, looks back at me. "Didn't your mother ever tell you not to pick up strangers?" His grin is toothy, lupine. "Drop by on your way back. Coffee is on me."

The door slams shut. In my rearview mirror, I watch a wolf lope into the fog.

Rocks

I'm a rock in an inner tube.
You're a rock skipping the water.
We started with enthusiasm,
with no idea of where
we might end up.
We're both in danger of sinking.

The danger could be
a blessing. We may find
secrets in the deep.
An old Roman road
going nowhere.
Gold coins gleaming
untarnished memories. Maybe
underwater caves
filled with crystals.

Maybe I'll find out
that inner tube
is actually my tummy.
Embarrassing.

All the better.
You'll float!
I'm the one
who will go under
onto a pile
of ancient stones
and sailor bones.

69

You will join the stones
and bones of our ancestors,
find gold and crystals left behind.
My legacy is
sunburn.

Spider webs

entrap my house,
tangle my memories,
snare my dreams,
perhaps snag
a trove of treasures
in the lattice of light
undefiled by dusters
just for me to find.

Spider webs
are lines of thought
that crisscross
and confuse.
They lead me
into other realms,
dissolving so
I can't return.

I search for ways
to bridge the gaps
mining miles of sticky plaque
as dreams and plans
and future hopes
tangle in the looping ropes.

My bridge is made
of sticky web
or maybe dental plaque.
Either way, my thoughts

fall through
the tangled loops
of fractured hopes and dreams.
I have to find another way
to jump the gaps
to find that treasure trove
of everything I want
this life to be.

Even if I have to ride
the spider's back to find
my rich rewards
for this tough life -
not what I left behind,
the dust -
the dust that beds
the bunnies in my head!

Spring is late

and flowers burst
light-speed to bask
in summer sun.
The bees are drunk,
they swerve insane
on nectar sweet.
Hollyhocks raise
their gypsy skirts,
last flowers, blooming
just in time to greet
The autumn winds.

I've dallied long enough,
delayed my day
to blossom.
The hollyhocks dance
with bees.
I primp
in the violet sun.

I'm late no matter what I do.
I think it's all the primping.
Better to be late, I say,
and show my blooms in style,
than slip through the back door
right on time
and no one see my petals.

The same old white gown
every season.
The Traditional Easter Lily.
Not the Stargazer
in her pink perfumery
and her clutter of butterflies.

Who needs a gown
when I can dress
in butterflies?
Who needs perfume
when busy bees
adorn me with
their pollen?

To do it all. Be it all.
Ready to impress the gardener.
Stand out. Stem strong.
Be the prettiest.
Bud at any age
with grace and ease.

Sunset Flood

The water rises,
snares my meadow blooms,
spills orange juice
on my flowered frock,
runs along the banks.
Rogue river!
I can't pursue you!
I am Ivy.

Orange juice
and pink popsicles

spill from the sky,
run through gutters
and summer sprinklers,
sweetening the end
of the day.

How can a love story begin
if I'm such a mess
from sunset to sunset?
Each spring my new wardrobe
is splattered by sherbet
at every day's end.
My rogue lover
eats my meadow.
I'm only here
for so long.

I may not be here long enough
to clean up the sherbet
mess I've made of love,
to clean the sticky fingerprints
off photos of us holding hands
and smiling at the days
far gone.

My meadow weathers
but I'm still held
by time flowing
and the sun lapping
the shore.

The Secret Life of Socks

The pair, a solid couple,
look alike, stink alike
have great jobs,
untethered
in leather factories,
but some never return
from work.

When we blame the washer
for eating our socks,
they're really out playing
and wining and dining,
forgetting our footsies
are freezing without them.

That creates jealousy
as some show up late
full of gaping holes
from threads yanked,
pulled out,
twisted around a cotton crew.

I don't want to know
what and where
they did with whom.
It's too much information.
I mend the holes
and call it good,
pretend it never happened.

You sound like Ms. Clean.
It doesn't bother you,
all the missing ones?
The mysteriously
mismatched pairs?
The pink ruffled anklet
tangled with the hiker one?

I wait six months
for mismatched mates
to magically appear.
If not, I toss
the whole lot out
and go on a sock
shopping spree.

Grab your purse.
There's a Sock Hop
Spree for Three
Overstock Sale.
at Victoria's Secret.

This Is No Earthquake

Where do we reconcile when
failures fracture, bridges break?
How do we speak
when contact crumbles?
How do we reunite
when our escape routes
vanish into void?

We think we've prepared
BPA-free water bottles,
holy books, battery chargers,
red wine, dark chocolate with
Red Sea salt, compendiums on
survival without love - or possibly with
never-failing love. In that case,
a camp tent large enough
for the dog.

The dog licks my face
to wipe away my worries
that I can't ever be prepared
for everything that happens.

Nor can I, nor could I,
Nor should I be immune
to life calamities.
All dark chocolate melts.
Contains arsenic. The hikes
to the perfect spot yield blisters.
Perfection has sores that
make us human.

That reminds me
to pack Pepto Bismol,
wet wipes for the
chocolate on my face,
and thick socks,
none of which
I'll ever use.

Maybe the Pepto Bismol
can repair those fractures
and collapsing bridges.
Maybe the wet wipes can wash away
the crumbled words in
failed communication.
Maybe thick socks
will comfort us on
those escape routes
into the void?

News flash: the void
is really a black hole
that sucked up my credit card.
I'm not buying a thing.

So, we return to your initial concerns
like mice on a treadmill
with no credit power, granted.
I have no answers. Only a camping trip
to escape rhetorical worry.

Too Much Snow

This winter buries me
in the blues,
each snowstorm blinds
my eyes with white.
Send a jar of sunshine
to pour on my cold skin.
I don't remember flowers,
bees, green grass.
The snow is endless.
Spring can never come
too soon.

Spring texts me.
"Running late, Hon.
At the mall.
Big sale at Victoria's Secret.
Got me some frilly pink socks
to go with my new floral day dress."

Spring is always late.
By the time she dresses
and pretties up her face,
big sister Summer
will arrive and melt
vain Spring with fiery
mid-day heat.

Sisters.
Always bickering.
Who's prettier?
Who's sexier?
Spring accuses Summer
of chasing Autumn
to disrobe.
Summer calls Spring
a cold fish
as Winter begs her
for more time,
but she rebuffs him.

Autumn doesn't join the fight,
instead, she runs away.
As she flees her sister's chase,
she scatters leaves
from all the trees.
Winter buries brittle leaves
under her white blanket,
plunder we'll discover,
thanks to Spring.
Instead of shoveling snow
we'll get out rakes
to clean up Autumn's
mess.

Spring's lament.
Dirty, crusty snow
draping her lush floral boutique.
Why is it always her job

to see to this sloppy mess?
And the nasty pop-up snowfalls
that smother her charm
just when she awakens!
Mother Earth's
Cinderella.

Spring forgets each year:
brittle leaves can fertilize,
winter snowmelt waters gardens,
And Summer?
Spring's still not talking to Summer.

Unconditional love

does not look back at me in the mirror.
The mirror is warped, or that body
is out of adjustment. I check my glasses
for smears and dirt. My reflection snickers.
"Doll, this is you in all your splendor.
Failed Fertility Goddess with bulges
in places that used to be slim.
Sags and bags and worn-out joints.
But it could be worse.

You could be a museum exhibit
in the Dinosaur Room."

My joints replaced
and displaced
as biohazard in a landfill
to be excavated
in a new millennium
by the great-great-greats
of today's Millennials.
When they reconstruct my face
from my fractured skull,
what age will I be?
Will I be cast as a lass
or a crone?

The crone in the mirror
is callous and cruel.
If she has to die,

she'll take everyone
with her.
We don't all go gentle
into that good night.

Wanna Play Marbles?

I'd play,
but I've lost my marbles.
Thought they were
in my purse. Last week,
I caught them rolling
down the hall
into my bedroom
under my bed,
hiding with the dust bunnies.

I lost my marbles,
they rolled out of my head
and out the door
to scatter sunlit reflections
my thoughts can't hold.

Maybe our marbles
will meet in the ivy
or under a tree
or in the gutter.
Knock around together
like pool balls.
Like startled memories.

Memories are pool balls
under startled ivy,
marbles once a child's toy,
forgotten in the gutter.
A trashman picks the marbles up

to give them to his baby boy.
Crystal balls refract the sun
of yet another childhood.

Where's the UPS guy

with my Amazon Prime delivery
I wanted two yesterdays ago?
Why don't you reroute your route
to bring it early for once?
Don't you know this is my fix?
I can't go to bed without it.

And why do you
deliver packages
on my back fence?
I find them clinging to the rim
in the rain no less.
I never did receive
"How to Dress a Fish" -
though it was "delivered".
You claim you never
make mistakes.
But now I miss
my poetry fix.

I know you're in a hurry
to get to your next stop,
or you might need
to take a bathroom break.
But please protect
my packages from
rain and snow
and theft, and
I'll keep you

from being fired
by giving you
good ratings.

Was this from you?
"Dear customer,
there's been a plague.
The supply chain has COVID.
Ships, planes, and trucks
are on life support.
Deliveries are limited.
Tissues, cough drops,
and poetry books
are on back order."

"Dear UPS Guy,
I understand you can't control
this COVID state of life.
Please find enclosed
some masks and gloves
and anti-everything spray.
Now get to work. Get me my stuff.
Don't you want to get paid?"

"Thank you for contacting us.
My name is B. Bot.
This call is being monitored
for the heck of it.
Mmmm. I see. I see. No way!
Let me transfer you
to the UPS guy.

We hope your issue
has been resolved."
Click!

Wouldn't it be great....

to awaken to
a shady country lane
lined with wildflowers.
A cozy cottage
whispering smoke
from the hearth.
A fruit tree
bearing promise.
Birds singing.
The sun shining.
Somewhere a brook
running clean
for child play.

I'd love to walk a country lane
that isn't paved with snakes,
to live in a cozy cottage
that someone else would clean,
to let someone else pick the apples
and prune the branches
while I go out for tea,
to watch my husband shoo
birds from the fence
where they leave their poop,
to stand in the sun long enough
to get my Vitamin D,
and to live far enough
from a babbling brook
that the mosquitoes stay away.

Not if you bequeath the fairies
bowls of rich cream and chocolates.
They'll bless you as long as you do.
No mosquitoes. No snakes. No storms.
No stinky poop on the car.
Only warm breezes, birdsong,
fields of flowers.

Warm breezes, bird song,
fields of flowers
I saw on a postcard once.
Right now, I'm shoveling
fields of snow,
and wishing winter
was over.

Remember the promise
that the clouds will clear.
The sun will come,
melting away
the dirty, crusty snow.
Fairies and fireflies
don't like winter woe.

Please send me fairies and fireflies
to melt the ice and snow.
If you don't have them, let me know.
I'll order them on Amazon.

Thoughts by Ken Tomaro

I don't think three sentences can describe what a great collection this is. There was a lot of wordplay I liked, but the poem, "If I was only," really sticks out.

I don't usually do current events, like mass shootings. I think writers jump on the bandwagon to bring attention to their own poetry rather than the actual event, but "No Words" was exceptionally well done and really brought to light the tragedy of the event, rather than you as the writers slyly saying, "Look at my marvelous poem...me, me, me!"

Many of these poems are so, so, so relatable, not wordsy or artsy just for the sake of being artsy, just good, down-to-earth poetry that will appeal to a large group of people. Honestly, it's the kind of writing that makes me want to punch a wall (for good reasons) thinking, why...can't...I...write...like...that?!

I got to "Road Trip" and I feel like punching so many walls, my arm will fall off. I could never do short stories/flash and I'm so jealous of yours. And the poems just kept getting better and better. I don't like anything, ever, but it is such a great collection!

I give it a solid 9 out of 10, only because there's no such thing as perfection. If you want a 10, it'll cost you $50 and 2 Chunky candy bars.

About the Authors

Barbara Leonhard is an internationally-known prize-winning poet and Pushcart nominee. She is especially indebted to *Well Versed 2021: A Collection of Poetry and Prose* and Spillwords Press for past honors. Her debut poetry collection, *Three-Penny Memories: A Poetic Memoir* (Experiments in Fiction, 2022), which is about her relationship with her mother, who suffered from Alzheimer's, is a best seller on Amazon. Barbara is also Editor for *MasticadoresUSA*. You can follow her at https://extraordinarysunshineweaver.blog/.

Nolcha's poems have been curated in *Lothlorien Poetry Journal, Alien Buddha Zine, Medusa's Kitchen,* and others. Her poetry books are available on Amazon and Dancing Girl Press. Nominee for 2023 Best of The Net. Editor for Open Arts Forum and Chewers & Masticadores. Accidental interviewer/reviewer. Faker of fake news.

Website: https://bit.ly/3bT9tYu

Facebook: nolcha.fox

Medium: @nolchafox_14571